Captives of Space & Time...

Poems, Lyrics and Riddles

Michael J. Nicholas

High & Tight Publications
Palm Desert, CA 92211
www.nickuvtyme@yahoo.com

Cover design by Michael J. Nicholas
Covert art by Baki Boquecosa @ Book Cover Arts

for
Vanessa
and
Izabella

proving angels exist,
even if there is no heaven

Acknowledgements

Mom, Dad, my brothers, my aunts and everyone in our loving family

All my friends. It's been about 50 years for some of us in B-Town... what the Hell?!

Pete and Duiven from A Random Drive- thanks for letting me be a part of your intense, musical trip

Jeremy, Larry and Sam of El Camino- a journey that included much more than music

Jim Churnin- a fellow musician and great friend. I always enjoy our conversations. Oh yeah, thanks for saving me from the 'Ether Rag'... hahahahaha

Cris Jefferies and Brian Dullum- two cool guitar cats that made room for an extra axe-slinger in their bands

Kenneth Lyon- a talented poet who has been a mentor and friend. Thanks for all the guidance and telling me, there are no set rules and make sure to have fun. You opened the door to the Writers Circle and Desert Poets, which gave me confidence to finally write this book

Rick Kenney and everyone at Desert Poets (Natalie, Marilyn, Rich, Barb, Sharon, Marvin, Florence and Ken). Everyone's wisdom, honesty and direction definitely helped with my focus and discipline

Marc Frederic (a.k.a. Mr. Whimsy) Carol Hazelwood and members of the Writers Circle. Your encouragement has been special and letting me serve on the Board of Directors is a duty I truly appreciate. Let's not forget the fun of the writers' salons that Carol graciously hosts

To all the players/ managers/ friends in Dark Lord Dynasty and The Stadium Freaks fantasy football leagues. A gracious shout out to Moc and Art for being the commissioners of D.L. and dealing with everyone's insanity. Some of us need straight jackets a little sooner than others! I can't forget to give special thanks to Jay and Brown, the leaders of S.F. who almost got us to 30 years. It was a sad day when the plug was pulled. R.I.P.

And, to a woman that a handful of these poems were inspired by… you know who you are

Table of Contents

A Race With Time

a Villanelle

Always in a race with time
When to go and when to turn
Trying to follow the signs

Killing it seems like a crime
Victim of changes we learn
Always in a race with time

Forcing us to toe its line
When to stop is my concern
Trying to follow the signs

Double nickels on a dime
When the rubber really burns
Always in a race with time

String theory might just be twine
When to flow, when to return
Trying to follow the signs

Perpetually on the climb
When atop, ash in the urn
Always in a race with time
Trying to follow the signs

How Fast is Fast?

Should I edit my thoughts
or let the phrases roll on out?
There are times when I have extra time
to rearrange concepts and words
during other conversation drills
syllables scale along as live notes
wondering if mood controls the tone
confidence surely has a play
affecting speed of delivery
while vibes from others entered
into the game called social hierarchy
may also be contending
to walk away with victory
knowing the pace of their words
was syncopated with their thoughts
making entries of brief happiness
until the next confrontation
where one's brain may be taxed
trying to understand which is better
having time to put items in a row
or flip the switch and tap into the now.

Anxiety could be the topic of communication
if not, my pen would own more ink.

Impatient Procrastinator

Need to have it
Can't wait for it any longer
Fixated on the wrong things
Not living in the moment
Mostly the future
Shmoozing with the past

Needing the task to unfold
Right when envisioned to take place
Ramps up stress
If the mission isn't a success

Putting life off
To pick out a perfect frame
One that will stand out
Amongst hopeful conceptions
Defining a being's worth

Neurotic signature blossoms
As you're that worried
About the passage of clock ticks
Upset, because you can't control the frenzy

Settled down to prioritize
A vital checklist of deeds
Placed in orders of dire
Might lift aged curses vexing
The Impatient Procrastinator

Black Glass

Slippery deals
From slick-black wheels
Where do I even begin

Obeying signs
Saving all my lives
Arriving in the near future

Seeing dark glass
Present becomes vast
I'm on the lighted side

Waving me on
Resisting all temptation
Common sense lights the path

Looking aside
Broke eye contact's line
For sure I'll win the stand-off

Crossing streets
Winners of urban feats
Medals earned one at a time

Cars will pass
Add escapes from black glass
A few more until I'm home

Telling It to the Ghosts

Not ready for Sunday
I was there but could not stay
Feeling life's breakaways
Telling it to the ghosts

On mind's plane to Sunday
I got on but could not stay
Plotting my breakaway
Selling it to the ghosts

Hiding out from Sunday
I looked back but could not stay
'round the block breakaway
Yelling it to the ghosts

Face to face with Sunday
Couldn't do nothing but stay
Peace of mind nowadays
Telling it to my ghosts

Lyrics, Melodies and Chords

a Sestina

Placing melodies over chords
Formulas to create songs
We can't forget lyrics
Which will stir depth
Combine thrill of sound
With the scope of poetry

Many are deaf to poetry
Not hearing a promise of words and chords
Locked out from vibrating sound
Obvious in their favorite songs
Strung together, emotional depth
More often cuffed by lyrics

The radio reads lyrics
Which started out as poetry
Until attached depth
A progression of backdrop chords
The development of songs
Random chimes disguised as plotted sounds

Depending on tones and sounds
Mixed with nerves of touchy lyrics
Can leave you with far out songs
Or enlightening poetry
Some as adding minor chords
To make major sympatic depth

Closing one's eyes can summon depth
Listen to lines spoken or the sense of sound
Subtle textures in groups of chords
Hidden intent within lyrics
You can find clarity in poetry
You can find voltage within songs

The spoken and played can both be songs
Relation decides personal depth
Steep with unspoken poetry
Wanderlust for audible sound
No better charge than writing lyrics
Then going à la mode with chords

Words designed always have sound
Echoes from the pith of lyrics
Songs formed when bred with chords

El Camino Blues

Verse 1

I can care less about credentials,
Never got any degrees.
Didn't play slap 'n tickle in the dorm room,
never had the chance.
Street-wise books
built me a life more real than
a Shakespearean tale.
Assigned reading in a class above
my then bank statement setback.
Future of promise,
strapped to years of manual labor,
stretching pennies
into copper wire,
a balancing act
of funds over the incurred.
Side hustles,
cushions of staying in the black,
can't go back
to the level you just left.
Spare gaps of time,
pick up a book,
read to escape
only if for a spot.

Verse 2

An outlet of verse and tones,
angry guitars and amplification.
Form a unit,
pen some tunes,
practice, practice practice.
Booking shows,
a battle of the bands,
invite your friends.
Money is a laugh,
a bar tab helps
even if it's flat tap.
Payment is when you play,
maybe keep the world at bay
long enough to forget
about the days
on either side of this one.
Tap into a vibe
with the other stage soldiers,
feeding off a crowd uncontrolled.

A Scanner's World

Lost my edge
social communication skills
now dull
compared to sharp tongues
sheathed yesterday

Modern man
multipotentialite
lots to get done
cruel technology
waits only for it's maker

Living free
proclomations of illusions
body and mind
one, two, sometimes three
beliefs become prisons

Polymath
adaptor, ending up alone
a past of classic parties
now writing my obit
needing to belong

Finding paths
reaching civilization
unlock cell-block gates
re-making first contact
the scanner is found

Checking Boxes

a Haiku

Hollywood has died
Checking boxes, checking out
New-age assertion

Pleasing everyone
Barely anyone is pleased
It's time to say cut

Woman

I like the way that you smile
The way you flick your hair
You put your hand in mine
And everything is all right

I love the way that you kiss
Your life on top of mine
And when you speak at night
I can hear you say

Oh, it's a crimson-colored sunset
A vision of two tales

You make me see myself
For who I really am
Even when you're wrong
You're always right

It's like ESP
The way you read my mind
And when you speak at night
I can hear you say

Oh, it's a crimson-colored sunset
Setting a tale for two

The way that you feel
It's when a man
Really loves a woman

Listen I do, yes I do, really do
Love you woman
Like no other

Now I really think
Think that I do
Love you woman

You and I
Passion and pantomime
Your warm body
Next to me and time

Passion and density
Pulsating data stream
Straight ahead
To the heavens of love
Your love, my love, our love

Oh, it's a crimson-colored sunset
A vision of two tales

Watching you watch me
Sending forever with that look in your eyes
And when you speak at night
I can hear you say

Oh, it's a crimson-colored sunset
Setting a tale for two

The way that you feel
It's when a man
Really loves a woman

Listen I do, yes I do, really do
Love you woman
Like no other

Now I really think
Think that I do
Love you woman

Oh woman
How many times are you
Going to make me say it

I really think
Think that I do
Love you woman

Seems to be Enough

Lyrics

Now that we are done,
did I let you go?
Did you just run?
Do I have to know?

Now there's no more fun,
did I make it snow?
Did I sink the sun?
Do you hear the crows?

But as the day winds down
why do I feel up?
Everything around me
seems to be enough,
it seems to be enough.
Getting rid of all the stuff,
it seems to be enough.

Now without a sound,
did I leave a trace?
Did I go around?
Do you need the space?

Now we are past blame,
did I say we're true?
Did you think the same?
Together we are through.

But as days wind down
why do I feel up?
Everything around us
seems to be enough,
it seems to be enough.
Getting rid of all our stuff,
it seems to be enough.

Catch and Release

Falling apart, without the structures of love
Simply finding that an empty companion won't fill an empty
hole
You need a soul that your fate knows about, someone who will
ease future's old

Want to go on a walk, hand in hand, talking
The energy of you, scents of your shampoo
I'll throw away sour feelings I had for you

My punishment for throwing it all away
The daily Eagle eats my heart and always returns
In my grasp, but another me didn't want it to last
What difference do outcomes mean now
Memories can never be taken away

Feeling Is Believing

Holding onto you
You're clinging to our love too
Trying to keep bright hearts
From states of freezing blue

Keep it together
Emotions change
Spells of weather
A heavy burden
A single feather

Both can see inside
Honest hearts that haven't lied
Now is our future
Always feeling alive

The bond is stronger
Than we both know
Finding out lasts longer
If there's lonely doubt
Hopefully honor

Garden of Walls

Living in a vector,
my life's garden of walls,
a bit short on the floor space,
yet endless ceilings tall.
Cascading within a chasm,
my life's garden of facts,
always much too real,
changing fate's impact.

All relationships inked,
from the blackbook of fate,
some familiar known names,
yet others blank slates.
Interactive beings,
encounters changing souls,
more future passing humans,
new contacts fill the bowl.

Divisions of all feelings,
never know which will show,
emotions once displayed,
memories now in the know.
Boundaries forge the lanes,
destiny lights the lamp,
sometimes you get to choose,
bright skies or dark and damp.

Being kept to the basics,
inside a windowless room,
difficult to find others,
there's always the saloon.
Rows of crops are ready,
harvest the needless lines,
wandering more freely,
once I removed those vines.

Living in a vector,
my life's garden of facts,
always much too real,
changing fate's impact.
Cascading within a chasm,
my life's garden of walls,
a bit short on the floor space,
yet endless ceilings tall.

Screams From Hell

What am I going to do with myself,
now that you've all dropped out of the game?

Pick it back up, start it again?
But I'm the only player that's going to roll the dice.

Taking that chance,
maybe go down in flames,
with a burning smile
as I do it my way.

Screams from Hell, I pretend they don't exist.
But I'm not the only roller,
who claims that they are deaf.

Random Subjects

Looking beyond
Which is in front of myself
Blind eyes fixated
On something further
Past the object ahead
Hardly in
My line of sight
Part of a gateway
To much deeper paths

Seconds of a gaze
Feel like journeys
Volumes of thoughts
Exceed single editions
Made of random subjects
Seeming depths unreal
As anything above
Which exists in the normal

I Saw It

Into madness I fell,
in psychosis I dwell,
feels like I've been gone
a very long time.

While bliss can be swell,
I won't see it 'till Hell,
somewhere I must of crossed
the wrong line.

Staring out,
I see it,
but you tell me,
it's not what you're looking for

Pointing out,
do you see it?
I already forgot
what I'm looking for.

Hand in the Cookie Jar

We're coming
Coming after you
Confession by projection

We have known
Known about you
Confession by projection

Don't look at me
The mirror is on the opposite wall
You can't throw blame
Fast enough to strike
The shining of the light

Following
Following you
Confession by projection

We'll always know
Know about you
Confession by projection

Stop looking at me
Your shadow is on the opposite end
Can't sling shame
Fast enough to cut
The shining of the light

Cable News Drunk

Psychotic break
Separating self
With a drunken reality
Twenty-four hour
Information access
Serves the sots
Delivering a fix
Comprised within fear
Of forever boogeymen
An addiction
To drama and suspense

"Another round of highballs!"

A need for ratings
Will dilute the facts
Orchestrating agendas
Will sway opinions
On the end of our seat
Waiting for a morsel
Curse the bad man
We can't leave the t.v.

"Another round of cocktails!"

Play it again, Sam
Tolerance won't give
Into acceptance
Of humbled concepts
Highway or your way

Storm off the playground
No part of a middle ground
You're your own blue-haired god

Another round of tipple!

Real People

Honesty
Respect
Find out
Social scenes
Required lies
Save face
Habit
Difficult
Kill switch

Opinions
Unwelcome
Still real
Deserves honesty
tact matters
Sugarcoating
Children and seniors
Feeding egos
Sick inside
Kind words
Buttery warm
Thin skin
Fleshy Jello
Wear a meter
Don't want one
Larger than my honesty

Johnny Lies

Johnny lies
Do you lie too?
Not authentic
Cheap-ass Ragu

Misinformed
Unaware
Slants from sole sources
Will leave you square

Echo chamber
Embrace today's chant
Can't hear meaning
Over the rant

Glory hole ethics
In it the same
They have no plans
Just bags of blame

Don't have to mend
Throw them a crutch
Non-for profits
Still profit a bunch

Chameleons
Transform with the day
Paint their canvas
A new gripe they say

Treadmill of Despair

Fast enough to pass you
But I'm falling far behind
Sharp enough to bleed you
But I can never gain the ground

As you can see
I'm running in place
The view never changes
Sometimes just the pace

As you can see
Running in one place
Outcome never changes
In this same 'ol race

Running
On the treadmill of despair
Time to get up
It's about that time

Running
On the treadmill of despair
Down on my luck
I'm down in the dumps
High enough to clear you
But I always get tripped up
Hot enough to burn you
But my clouds block out the rays

As you can see
I'm running in place
The view never changes
Sometimes just the pace

As you can see
Running in one place
Outcome never changes
In this same 'ol race

Running
On the treadmill of despair
Down on my luck
I'm down in the dumps

Running
On the treadmill of despair
Time to get up
It's about that time

A Bowl of Black

a Haiku

Coyotes howl
Sun gives way to the dark night
Seeing the stars scream

As a bowl of black
Filled atop flickering specks
I am always small

High and Tight

The lights go down
and it's time to do her show
Like a birthday
I always get my wish
Sitting in the back row
'cuz I just may lose control

I couldn't be wrong
Oh no
I know that I'm right
Uh huh
This little girl's set up
High and tight

The lights come up
It's time to hit the switch
Like my birthday
She comes bringing gifts
My eyes are spinning
'cuz I just lost all control

I couldn't be wrong
Oh no
I couldn't be right
Uh huh
This little girl's set up
High and tight

High and tight
Hot and bright
She's set up
High and tight
I couldn't be wrong
I know that I'm right
This little girl
Is set up
High and tight

All Out of Coins

When the boatman comes calling
can't seem to get away.
Could it be a selfish story?
Got to keep on movin',
   "baby, I can't stay."

One of those lonely, summer nights
when it's obvious I end up alone.
My fear is knockin' and it never seems
I feel like I'm at home.

Maybe I should make up my mind,
just get through with it.
Get on the tip of this life,
or just get off it.

There's a way to play the game,
in and out of the cold ground.
Be the big fish of the sea
in the shadow of a city
that never peaks.

Walking up and down the moors
when you hear driftwood creak.
Angels will abandon you
in the loneliest of places.

Outside the Box

Boredom and complacency crept into his still mind.

As soon as the shoelaces
were pulled tight
the jacket's zipper
was due north,
he faced the door.

A gray-day's threshold
now at his back,
impatient feet
propelled him forward,
while composed winds
unconcerned
his state of being.

Emotional Tampon

Emotional tampon
Soaking up your sorrow
Tears of today and tomorrow
Getting pulled down with the ship
A melancholy abyss
Sucks you down the quicksand
Keeping all your days full
Trying to ride the bull
Getting thrown off into space
A dark and lonely place
Next to beings of light
Who never know you're there
Until you make them care
Getting annoyed by the woes
That they never chose
To complicate their day
Wanting smiles without clowns
More sunshine and less frowns
Getting far from the octagon
Emotional tampon

Don't Blame Me

Lyrics

You're so cold to the touch,
why do I even try?
When you speak to me,
how come you bring me down?
I've played your games,
yes I have.

There came a day I was judged,
watched by your evil eye.
Finally, it's become enough,
don't blame me, I tried.

When you get in the wrong mood,
out comes your spooky tooth.
When you've out-stretched the size,
out come the lies and flies.

There came a day I was judged,
Watched by your evil eye.
God damn, it's become enough,
Don't blame me, I tried.

So I'm on my own,
for about a week.
Are you thinking about,
me taking you back?

37

There came a day I was judged,
watched by your evil eye.
Much too much, it's become enough,
don't blame me, I tried.

So tell me this,
do you tear when you cry?

Pretty Green Eyes

Lyrics

I tried and tried,
still, she said *"no."*
What was on her mind,
she wouldn't let me know.

Flashes of days,
she knew but chose not to say.

All I want
Is to squeeze her hand
And to tell her
Please trust me
But how could she
A devil's smile
Is always the same
Even coming
From a winged angel

Pure, she seemed,
yet dirty as dusk's streetlight.
Seeking and shrieking,
along we must pass.

I want to look at her pretty, green eyes.

Tell me an epic of sorrow and mistrust,
I can only soak up, that pain you feel.
It's nothing to,
your pretty, green eyes.

They're everything I have

4th Dimension Protocol

Viewing the 4th dimension
Not with those eyes in your head
Taking more to perceive
All which is really out there

Spectrums and color charts
Not seen by the eyes in your head
Dismissing hard realities
Accepting what you've known

Angles you can't decipher
Not by the space in your head
Which is in which is out
Are you coming not going

Obviously a part of it
Not known by the brain in your head
Unable to sense those structures
Doesn't mean they aren't there

Viewing the 4th dimension
Not with closed eyes in your head
It's taking more to believe
All which is really out there

My Brain is a Chemistry Set

a Rondeau

Mixing chemicals within my brain
Stirring the pot hits like a train
A bunch of fun was prescribed by me
The dark stuff passed out by my M.D.
Two to one I'll be going insane

Taking one pop can't lead to fame
Invite a carry-on when you board the plane
Ready for take-off the sights we'll see
Mixing chemicals

A concoction of corrupters seeps through the veins
It's all my fault, doctor's half the blame
Now I take supplements, bark from every tree
Fighting off hands of time, just turned fifty-three
Even when you're dry, it always seems to rain
Mixing chemicals

I'm in Love With My Waitress

I'm in love with my waitress,
should I leave a tip
or a kiss?
Did she bring me
the menu for love,
after leading me
from door to booth?

I'm under the spell of my waitress,
beauty flowing out of
the kitchen mist.
Does she feel
energy around us,
as I sense the
vibrating Universe?

My waitress could probably care less,
if I'm distressed,
an absolute mess.
Another patron of
no consequence,
needing confidence
for conversations.

My waitress smiled with a fondness,
reciting specials
with a demure press.
Taking my order with

a pixie's playfulness,
less distressed,
now we can talk.

I locked eyes with my waitress,
should I look away,
maybe persist?
Is she thinking about
our ocular grip,
which will prove to her
my honest intent?

I'm in love with my waitress,
should I leave a tip
or a kiss?
She brought me the check
phone number on back,
her sweet smile spoke,
"let's leave it to fate."

My E-Bike Does 33

a Haiku

Miles per hour
My e-bike does thirty-three
I average five

Battery is strong
Speed limit is thirty-five
I walk a good pace

Seventy-five pounds
Throttled beast of gray steel
I'm at two hundo

Looking up at Mountain Tops

A Golden Shovel after Pink Floyd's "Time"

Clocks are now digital, can't hear the ticking
seconds since I moved away
to an arid land where the
sand is fine and the moments
of sunshine are truly that
abundant, enclosed mountains make
up half the sky as you look up
towards peaks that only a
hawk can grasp, sharpening dull
claws on moon rocks of his day.

Hoping we could re-start raptures, you
unwillingly changed the course, not wanting to fritter
commitments, responsibilities and
a lifestyle of security, nay waste
time worrying about reimagining the
future, where anxious hours
of assembling us, while taking in
past selves, enacts an
amount of doubt, even if off-hand
motives part without finding a way.

On my walks, random rocks I'm kicking
two miles ahead and back around,
deep in thought, my feet are on
the concrete, cascading across a
greenbelt towards the lonely piece

of structure I call home, 2x4's of
missed dreams cemented to the ground
and I can't believe the roof hasn't caved in
under the crushing weight of your
strayed smile, back at your home
across the country in E-town.

Days blend together as I'm waiting
to hear some sort of signal, for
myself to be considered someone
that you've forever been seeking or
to fill a void and add something,
making you complete if not to
give me a chance to show
how high I could bring you
placing us on top of the
mountains out my way.

The Mind Light

a Rondeau

Switching the mind light to *always on.*
Voices whisper, *"sleep's the biggest con."*
Could I be dreading today will end?
How do I make tomorrow my friend?
Fighting insomnia's telethon

Brain can't stop the flow of electrons,
blaming the devils, imps and gorgons.
Can't we message sleep and hit *send?*
Switching the mind

Slide out of bed and try the futon,
My eyes closed can see the neon.
Can counting backwards be the true mend?
Will hours fretting make the mind bend?
Hijacked, sane pathways of my neurons,
Switching the mind

Whacked Out Dreams

My consciousness drifts to the other side.
Don't want to go, but know that I have to.
Always shadowy, the doors of entry are unsettling origins to lost hallways,
connecting scenes of the past with twisted possibilities of tomorrow.
Devoid of reason, these scenes beam chills down the spine,
increases my heart rate,
makes me sweat.
It all stems from stress.
If you control your day,
the night won't have its claws through you.

A cast of characters from life's playbill,
make their cameos, read their scenes,
with newcomers, good and bad.
Sometimes I'm an onlooking drifter,
empty dialogue in my script,
not envisioned for me.

Trying to get out of rooms,
running away if I can.
Looking for objects I can't find,
my brain wants it that way.
Settling vendettas made by those trapped in circuits.
Some angry, some sad, some happy.
Do I control in a way, their emotions,
the moods, the love, their aggressions?

Featured players, known and needy,
will edge me towards my wake-up.
Others give me a reason to stay,
only if a tiny bit longer,
maybe to see how mirages plays out
on the big screen behind my eyes.

I'd ask who is creating these whacked out dreams,
I've figured out it's me.

The Cycle Will Never End

Traveling aside
A cold beam of light
Lighting up horrors
Once hidden by night
The cycle will never end

Orb of scorched fire
Saves half the time
Timing won't matter
When omens arrive
The cycle will never end

Sun along with spells
Witches see both set
Setting up meetings
With demons not met
The cycle will never end

Eyeing star light
Cast angry shadows
Shadowing villains
Stalking the meadows
The cycle will never end

Scenting a specter
Pacing empty dark
Darkened devil found
Dogs too afraid to bark
The cycle will never end

Hear the tortured werewolf
Screaming at the moon
Moon-phase always constant
His fate is doomed
The cycle will never end

We Seen Them

"It's like there's some kind of a hallucinatory flu going around.
People seem to get over it in a day or two.
All I can do is treat the symptoms."
- Dr. David Kibner
Invasion of the Body Snatchers'

Staring
at a backyard tree
a buddy and I
late May breeze
dull moonlight illuminating
ghouls of chalk-white skin
serving
saucer-sized pupils
which gape at the growth
spawning
from fertile Earth
towards the inviting sky
where space snakes hide.

Fixated
we remained
lined up our sight
straight ahead to the structure
that we knew was beyond us
yet, directly in front of us
giving
the chilling illusion
spelled out indirectly
the total insignificance

to where we actually fit
inside the cosmic coat
which warms us
until secondary passages
were conceived
every thought or three
elating how everything is connected.

And to think
there's a tree out there
which helped these spores grow
from its shade and nutrients
so we could chew them and laugh
then maybe
buy a ticket somewhere
to a place close by
still very far
once the fungus
had shifted gears
leading us out
to the backyard
with intent to stare at the tree
delivering a message
with scattering gazes
including anxious, sheepish grins
using a pair of human vessels
the mushroom maker greets
his cross-country cousin.

Laughing at the Insane

Monkey cage
Crazy rage
Throw away the key

Wars we wage
Crazy rage
Patient zero is me

Laugh at something scary
You're the one who's crazy
What side of the line are you on

Cry at something real
You're unaware of the deal
We know what side you're on

Where Are You?

My friend chose to ride out
The dark, long path
Long path to the end

Rather of seen a shooting star
Light up our sky

Went on a trip
Lonely as shadows on the moon
The journey was forever
Ending came too soon

Getting lost
When your people are around
Head in flight
Feet slipping on the ground

Leaving for that next stage
Prefer to travel alone
Wish you wanted us to help
Help you move that stone

The long, dark path
She calls like a siren
A seductive song
Until you've locked eyes
With the black wren

If the light shines
Wherever you happen to be
We are waiting for you
Where the sun hits
Sobbing willow trees

Vociferously Obvious

Lack of attention span
Creating restlessness
Lesser of two evils
More of the similar situation
Interlocking horns
With glowing eyes of crimson
Growling a sales pitch
A platform built on greed

Lack of attention span
Stirring the pot of angst
Join the opposition, modern tribalism
More of the sinister situation
Persuasive tongues
Perfect, slicked back hair
Preaching guilt trips
Slinging stale nationalism

Lack of attention span
Planting the seed of despair
Blindly becoming what they want you to be
More of the sadistic situation
Slimy smiles showing teeth
That glow bright white
Promising you a today
While stealing your tomorrow

The Beans Have Spilled

a Villanelle

Choices were made in private
Back on those special days
Before we lost etiquette

Peaceful before the onset
Lost in summer haze
Choices were made in private

Dad dreamed of Corvettes
Men driving Stingrays
Before we lost etiquette

Heard about the great reset
Going one of two ways
Choices were made in private

A medicated outlet
All sides own a phrase
Now that we lost etiquette

Open mic mindset
Families set ablaze
Choices were made in private
Before we lost etiquette

Down by the Lake

Bastards of fire
Come with me
Put out your flames
In the sea

They'll teach you to know
About the way
Conformity my friend
Slipping away

Bastards of fire
Wait and see
Fires burning down
The big city

Light a match
And be like them
But you gotta be you
Now and then

Down by the lake
There's a path to take
You have to take control
Wooden stakes and rattle snakes
You have to save your soul

Bastards of fire
Get there for free
There's gold in the garden
Treasure in the tree

Get the booty
Set sail home
Don't have to leave
You're free to roam

Bastards of fire
Freedom's a treat
Take it for granite
And you'll lose your seat

Own your life
Expressions true
Don't be them
When you have you

Down by the lake
There's a path to take
You have to take control
Wooden stakes and rattle snakes
When *will* you find your soul

A little Bit of This

This and that
A tit for tat
Why can't you let the past go
Back to where it all belongs
Today won't reset yesterday's wrongs
Memories pass by in slo-mo

This and that
A red-eyed bat
Sucking blood from my last nerve
Draining leftover patience
My anxiety is your science
The child in time you serve

This and that
A buck-toothed rat
Gnawing away at my being
Chewing off the meat
Routine feedings are the feat
Ignoring silent telephones

This and that
A one-eyed cat
Half the romance you couldn't see
Not fitting into your mold
Unlike the love you were sold
If she only understood it couldn't be

Kicking the Booze Hound

Why do we drink? Run, run away from myself as fast as I can. I'm the scariest being I don't want to be. Alter ego needs to come out and play, it's more fun anyway... and the liquor pigs like him a lot.

Slows you down after stressful days of needless tasks and forgotten dreams. Gotta find the right zone without going all Mr. Hyde. As the stresses rise, so does the body count of shameful liquor store purchases, who quickly lost their lives.

Radio Rot

A child growing up
in the backseat amusement park
of our family's sedan.
FM radio called to me
an audio trance
like the siren of the sea.
Now, not so much

Attitude and Energy

Attitude and energy,
forces of motivation,
the torches of creation.
When you feel that inner glow,
Does it give you the chills?
Does it give you your thrills?

Action, not words,
hear what I do.
Listen up,
Here's my next move.

Attitude, it's not what's said,
the things you do
give you your edge.
Energy, coming from within,
appease the power,
release your grin.

Understand, and turn it on,
do it for you and do it for me,
do it for them, then you'll see.
When you feel that inner glow,
it *will* give you the chills,
it *will* give you your thrills.

It's not what you've done,
it's what you're doing now.
Touch the Sun
as you take your bow.

A Tale From the Lost and Never Found

The home underneath my feet
Thirteen years of being lost
Above sorrow's surface
Trying to steer a truck
Built on depression's weight
Away from a collision course
Constructed against framed memories
And today's anguish, with hopes
Concerning future disillusions

Tears no longer found
I'm too dry to cry
Three of us remaining
Bound by an element of her aura
Nomadic in our paths towards solace
Calamitous work of heartache and kismet
Disseminating loss in divergent states
An enduring routine
Healing sometimes impedes
Needed bond strengthening
Possibly afraid to get closer
Always feeling great loss
Maybe in waiting
Around the corner
Further weakening a will
To start the day with a smile and can-do

She left because she had to
Some say chose, but what did they know
Judging covers only solicits ideas
Of what's contained within
Outcomes already known
Blind the eyes to viewing realities

"Sometimes", feels like yesterday
"Also", feels like right now
Pain, can slowly drip
Downward from the brain
Caught into a drain which
Always remains concealed
Breaching the door to
Today's spellbound visions
From that lost angel
Gliding high in the clouds
Unaware, grisly grips of demons
Were tasked to keep her down
Forever on Earth's mortal plane

Searches for solemn good-byes
My dreams play out as
Undirected stage acts
Lacking rhyme, reason
Even needed conclusion
To quench manic tendencies
Of self-sabotage
When relating towards
New and possible romances
Wounds and scars hidden
Beneath flesh are never visible
Upon first glance, appearing
Evidently more distinct
As steep stares add up
Pushing away chances
At achieving wholesome love

Clinging onto days that seemed more innocent
Though, they weren't really at all
Just living in one's comfort zone
When the unexpected
Occurred more frequently
Than I sometimes remembered

Finally rise, daily onward
Splash water against my face
Diluting the dusty tears
Which drip down to the floor atop
The home underneath my feet

A Part of Your Destiny

A part of me
A part of another
Biology soup
An arbitrary mix

Your destiny
Fused together
Already built
Still growing young

A part of me
A part of another
Her traits or mine
Time will know

Your destiny
Blood of your father
Biology soup
Fused together

Atom's Child

Denounced my baptized faith
Eighteen years old I believe
Not in a "screw you" way
Rather, this isn't a movie for me

My family avoided church
Going only when beckoned
By white weddings and black funerals
Appearances only for others

When I last put down the good book
The thud broke grandma's heart
Even dad called me a heathen
Knowing he was just steps behind

What I finally fell into
I was always a preceding part of
Fathered by the Universe
Mothered in time by Earth

Random chaos seems to make more sense
Disarray becomes random order
Letting it all self-create
Nature assimilates

They told me I was crazy
Simply, new-age hippy crap
What did they know anyway
Hiding behind gods and guilt

Excuses to validate sins
Judgements cast upon others
In tandem with imposed shame
Sold by frauds in posh robes

Collection plates are soon emptied
Mirroring plates of the always hungry
Adorning trinkets in pure gold
Does your savior think this saves souls?

Walls of selected faiths built higher
Glad I can see over the top
Masters and minions of mind-theft temples
Unable to control my stainless thoughts

Zealots echoing peace
Conversations centuries old
Do they want to cross the finish line?
Is there even a race?

Knowing every atom is connected
Respect for all beings expected
Universal things, Pantheists believe
Yet the enslaved say, the free are naïve

Love and Rockets

by Michael J Nicholas

Stranded in space
A planned week
Becomes a year
Uncertain of the rendezvous
Bringing us home

Do we dare try
Chancing our trip
Cradled in the confines
Aboard questionable technology
That carted us here?

Can't we leave now?
Why must we wait?
Soulless administrators
Creating zero-gravity children
Shifting their pawns

A new frontier
Men, owning will and wisdom
Devising a plan
Free us from partisan bondage
See the beam of assurance

Test rockets launched
Trials made and approved
Perfecting a vital rescue

Many have forgotten about
Maybe just don't care

Mad genius
Mind of our time
Assured duties can be done
Proving his triumphs will be his payment
Benefit mankind

Phases complete
Mission ready, go
Fueling excitement
Remembering no one left behind
Our rescue is launched

Climbing towards
Heaviest skies
Rocket pulls through
Curtains of atmosphere
Eye on the prize

All systems go
Knock at our door
Fresh-faced visitors
Mission will bring us home
Didn't think twice

Leaving that scene
Of failures turned crimes
Relieved we have splashdown
All smiles waiting to thank
The daring engineers of Space-X

Frequencies of the Universe

a Villanelle

Emerging from the Singularity burst
An endless trek across oceans of time
Connecting frequencies of the Universe

Witnessing shock waves of this dimension's birth
Blinded, profound possibilities thrive
Emerging from the Singularity burst

Imposing things seen, could I be the first?
Colored spectrums against veils of white
Connecting frequencies of the Universe

Backdrops cede black as the Grim Reaper's hearse
Claiming dark voids once affecting all bright
Emerging from the Singularity burst

Gravity causing a vacuum and a lurch
Starshine created with no end in sight
Connecting frequencies of the Universe

My cosmic, space-quest has ended on Earth
Stars, planets set to deep sky
Emerging from the Singularity burst
Connected frequencies of the Universe

Poem Index

Author Details

Michael J. Nicholas was born in Chicago on June 13th, 1971. No, it wasn't on a Friday but referring to the "perpetual black cloud" that he claims to follow him overhead, you would think that he was. While working in the trades and home remodeling field, his passion lied in music, where he was a guitarist and songwriter in various musical acts.

Michael has two lovely daughters and currently lives a semi-private life in the Coachella Valley of California, where he loves the mountains, big skies and intense heat of the 'always sunny' desert.

Just as in life, *Captives of Space and Time* is a quick read. 52 poems from a guy who wants to tap the brakes and enjoy the slices of life between yesterday and tomorrow.

www.ingramcontent.com/pod-product-compliance
Lightning Source LLC
Chambersburg PA
CBHW070553030426
42337CB00016B/2483